To My love,

Enjoy!

Jettie Manscing McWilliams

Music in the Wind

A Collection of Poetry

by

Jettie Manning McWilliams

Westview Publishing Co., Inc.
Nashville, Tennessee

First Perfect Bound Edition December 2004

ISBN 0-9755646-8-4

Printed in the United States of America

Acquisitions Editor, Hugh Daniel

Cover design and other pre-press by Westview Publishing Co., Inc.

Westview Publishing Co., Inc.
8120 Sawyer Brown Road, Ste. 107
Nashville, TN 37221
http://www.westviewpublishing.com

Dedicated
to my family

POETRY IS BEAUTY

"——Poetry is music for my song.
the peak of glory, surpassing splendor,
tumultuous joy, oft times depths of sorrow.
Poetry is love ethereal
in praise of God, the Saints, the sky,
Heaven, the earth, and you and I. ——"

Introduction

Life seems a journey through time, a gift of a small niche in a place and moment on this planet earth. Our experiences are varied, vast, and depend on many factors: country where we live, culture, family, era of time, forces shaping our lives over which we may seem to have little control. Yet we all share certain wonderful capabilities such as free will, and the power of thought. We approach each situation from our own vantage point, and perspective.

This book is a collection of poetry written since my retirement from university teaching. It is more often a reflection and celebration of my own life experiences, but at other times it is an attempt to understand and make sense of the tragedies and triumphs of real and imagined friends in both today's world and in the past. As I look back on this joyous, and sometimes tumultuous, journey certain moments and events take center stage.

It is my sincere wish that the readers will find some poems that speak to their hearts, and many to which they can relate. We may share similar experiences. Through poetry we can communicate best our deepest feelings, hopes and memories.

"—— Poetry speaks for my spirit and my soul,
    reflecting the images I behold
      in dreams."

Contents

Changing Seasons

A GOOD MORNING

Awakened by a long-forgotten melody,
I quickly sit upright.
Who can that be?
"You're talking to the wind,"
An unseen voice answers me.

The daybreak comes early
this time of year.
Streaks of sunlight in the window
promise a day of good cheer.
I close my sleepy eyes gently,
I'd like to hear the end of the melody

𝕏

WALK NEW PATHS

There is much to say,
after so many years,
to break the silence
once deemed by us golden.
How can I explain,
in mere mortal terms,
circumstances, luck, and sorrow
that pervaded the times?

Suffice it for now.
Let's look to the future,
as we travel the journey

to unspoiled lands and dreams.
Let us be friends again,
and walk new paths,
and jump the hurdles
that brought us together.

≈

AN APRIL WALK
~ To Lauren ~

"Let's go for a walk.
It is such a nice day,
we can feed the ducks.
They're right on the way
to the shiny green belt
and the stony little creek
where the winter snows melt,
and the spring rains meet."

The April sunshine felt
cheerful, yet concealing,
the day a rare treat.
The sky was blue, revealing.
In the fast moving stream
the ducks' sounds repeating
as they went for a swim.

"Let's cross on the plank."
Nature probably didn't plan
to play a capricious prank,
but the board flew up
and I slid into the mud.
The water felt icy cold,
my clothes began to soak

4

"Here, Grandma, take my hand."
My seven-year old granddaughter
seemed to take command.
Looking around, I could find
no stones or surface to get
a firm hold.
"Steady, you can do it."
Her voice sounded bold.

My feet touched the ground,
I garnered my strength,
her energy had no bound.

She looked at my shoes,
that before had been clean,
my mud filled clothes,
then she broke into a grin.
"When compared to the duck,
it all seems so mean,
it can swim in that muck!"

※

BIRDSONG AND CHILD

Perched with eyes wide open and wings outstretched,
The seabird searched the surrounding sand.
The tiny girl walked slowly and confidently
Along the shoreline with absolutely no dread.
Smiling and chattering, she held her mother's hand.

What could be more exciting and fun!
A day at the beach, wet swimsuits and shells,
A time to relax, recreation brings pleasures unforeseen.

"Come, Mommie, it is time for a family run!
Catch me, here I go, faster and faster up the sand hills!"

Bells on her shoelaces sound much like the chimes
Ringing and mingling with bird song in the wind.
The sun shining gloriously on Mother and daughter,
The hint of raindrops calls forth a rhyme,
Ever looking forward, life's music and laughter blend.

Copyright 2003

ॐ

REMEMBERING SOUNDS OF SUMMER

The happy days of summer are all too fleeting.
The gleeful laughter of school children at play
And birds of many species sing joyful melodies, treating
Listeners to the marvelous sounds of summer. An array.
always enticing, of nature's symphony.

I remember.

The lofty dreams and empty thoughts of the small child
Were melded together by the shattering thunder
and then soft patter of rain.
I remember the animal mating calls in the wild,
And the gentle cadence of the whistle of a lone train
in the far and vulnerable distance.

Copyright 1996

ॐ

6

SHADOWS OF SUMMER

The flowers and plants put on a mighty show,
with every hue and color of summer's rainbow.
As the sun casts a blanket strewn with light,
the earth rejoices before the on coming night
when the stillness prevails.

I am reminded of pleasant days so bright,
wondering if the fickleness is just for spite,
by the drizzle of rain in the early day.
or just another instance of summer's way
of making our dreams always elusive.

❧

FAREWELL, SUMMER

Farewell. lazy days and nights of awesome wonder,
family picnics, camp fires under the haunting moon.
filled with mysteries of earth and universe to ponder,
I am struck by summer's frailty, to be gone so soon.
opening the door for the next season.

Although school days and childhood friends
I sometimes see as an intrusion upon my summer fun,
it is time for change, and the autumn blends
my day time dreams, and my eternal need to run
with the new challenges of the future.

❧

SOME MORNINGS ARE LIKE THAT

I feel the coming of a poem.
Some mornings are like that.
The cool crispness of the wind
penetrates into the core of my mind
to the vestige of poetry giving birth.

Oh, who has not experienced the warmth
of the sun on a still autumn dawn
filtering into the multi-layers of tension,
replacing them with the beauty and calm
of a morning both glorious and inspiring.

The poetry deep inside my heart feeling
gently nudged from the hidden spaces
midst the fear and sadness of my being.
My spirit brings forth the melody within
and rhythm of a song as my soul awakens.

♌

LATE SEPTEMBER

My eyes search the distant tomorrow
For signs of hope in my melancholy.
The darkened clouds continue to cover
The lingering warm days of summer,
September's reluctant departure.

The late September sunflower
Lazily sways in the twilight breeze,
Seeming almost out of place,
Trying to lift its' bright yellow face

8

Mirroring my plea for harmony.

Then along comes the symphonic melody,
Out of the dim and distant tomorrow,
Filling the air with sounds of laughter.

There's really no need for sorrow,
The children are at school, it's late September.

Copyright 2004

❧

OCTOBER MASKS
~ *To Daniel* ~

October brings frost,
and bright colored leaves
that fall to the ground
from beautiful trees.

Farmers gather pumpkins
for the children to enjoy,
carve into happy faces
for a Halloween ploy.

Witches and goblins
go out on the street,
often scare the neighbors
for a trick or treat!

October can be fun,
as the weather turns cool,
folks wearing masks
old friends to fool.

9

Autumn is very nice,
wear sweaters and shoes,
children are told
as they go off to school.

Winter will come soon,
Jack Frost foretells.
Enjoy the warm sun
before the sleigh bells!

❧

OCTOBER'S SHADOWS

October is a much- celebrated time of year.
We venture outside to enjoy the waning ways
of bright sunshine and summer's long days.
Neighbors wave across well-groomed lawns
soon to be frostbitten and fading into browns.

We pause for a brief while, maybe shed a tear.
reflecting on what changes have come around.
Sons and daughters have children of their own,
this house is no longer our cozy family home.
Should we move to a smaller and safer place?

The grandchildren often come for a short stay.
They liven up this place, bringing laughter and joy
to our hearts, reviving long forgotten memories
of children laughing, playing with cherished toys.
Perhaps it can't hurt for us to stay a little longer.

After all, there is no rush to move away.
This old house is still a family treasure.

Do you think a little paint, a bright sofa or chair
will fix it up like new and bring fresh air?
A couple more years should give much pleasure.

We linger, gazing across the still green meadows.
The squirrels will come soon, the nuts to gather,
flowers will splash color, a last glorious display.
With stunning grace, life touches October's shadows.

❧

PHANTOM ON ICE

I had planned a trip
to the mountains today.
The weather forecast was a shock,
"High winds and light snow.
Temperatures will hover
somewhere around the freezing mark."

"Travel advisory,"
the announcer had to say.
"Roads will be slippery.
If your trip isn't necessary . . ."
Forced to cancel my plans,
now my day looked stark.

What would happen
to my shattered dream?
I needed a glittering break
from my bleak routine.
Maybe tomorrow travel can resume,
I felt a renewed spark.

I conjured up in my mind

a snow clad mountain stream,
and a stunning scene.
The winds would subside
just enough for me to glide,
a solitary phantom on ice!

ॐ

WINTER DREAMING

The winter snows came sudden this year.
Couldn't figure out why I woke so early.
I sensed an aura of joy and fear,
the room was chilled with an air of mystery.
I pressed my nose against the window glass,
while no one stirred in the entire house.

The white snow brought an awesome glare.
Chirping and singing, the snowbirds danced.
.I could see as through a torch's flare,
still in the dawning, I watched entranced.
Were they calling for me this wintry day
to join them in their mystifying play?

A noise distracted me from my whim.
A squirrel jumped from a very tall pine,
needles spraying a splash of snow from a limb.
Scurrying forth ahead of the line,
watching and looking, acorn in hand,
she seemed to know the lay of the land.

Reluctantly, I moved away from the dream,
and focused my mind on the cares of the time.
I had made plans and must now beam

my thoughts and muscle toward work and clime.
The driveway must be shoveled, the car I must start.
There's much to do, I know in my heart.

Snow brings serenity, escape, and cold,
Snowbirds and squirrels for a short while.
Dreams of substance, some so bold,
sharing my sacred passion for style,
come dazzling into my innermost part.
There is much to do, I know in my heart.

❧

REMEMBERING CHRISTMAS AT AN EARLIER TIME

Come with me. Let's take a look
at a Christmas morning of my childhood.
You hesitate? Here, take my hand. See?
The little girl by the Christmas tree.

As a child of the Great Depression,
I didn't expect lavish gifts.
Yet I rushed to the tree with much anticipation.
The magic of Christmas was alive and well.

We hung our stockings by the fireplace
very much like the children of today.
The merriment of Christmas in the air,
the smells and sounds were everywhere.

The magical moments of delight
filled us with wonder and surprise.
An orange and an apple couldn't be beat
stuffed in our stockings ever so neat.

13

A nut or two filled out the toe.
We shook it thoroughly, making sure carefully,
not to miss any gumdrops or perchance little toy
Santa had placed. What a thrill! What a joy!

Hard times, little money, few frills,
we knew the Christmas story well,
how Jesus was born at Christmas time.
Each year Christmas seemed more sublime.

≈

SHADES OF LOVE

Love in its infancy
is an exciting thing.
A fleeting glance, a tender touch,
meaningless whispering,
still the smile means so much.

Love in its youth
goes out of bounds.
Trying to contain emotion
seems useless, adults have found.
Joyous moments are filled with passion.

Love blossoms into maturity.
Two hearts beat as one.
Loving experiences with the family
bring happiness and fun,
as time moves forward swiftly.

The elderly couple hold hands
in the lingering twilight.
The parade of youth in love pass
observing the couple with wonderment.
Does true love time outlast?

≈

SOARING AFAR

Soaring, sailing, I watch
the clouds drift softly
into the often capricious sky.
Musing, dreaming, images
encompassing more than dots,
squares and circles emerge
through endless distance.

Unfamiliar, mind boggling visions
dance through serene horizons
of seascapes, and landscapes,
where go you and I?
A journey through a small segment of space,
we on this planet soar
in nature's eternal embrace.
Tilting my head and soaring afar,
I witness a moment of God's eternity.

જ

Just Before The Sun Rising

JUST BEFORE THE SUN RISING

I awake to the splendor of early morning
just before the sun rising.
The song of the meadowlark
energizes my enthusiasm for the day's work

I awake to the splendor of early morning
just before the sun rising.
I fully embrace the joy and ecstasy
of planning my day with family.

The splendor of early morning
just before the sun rising
brings cause for celebration
continuing until each day's completion.

☙

RAYS OF LIGHT

The sun's rays of early light
are glistening over the rising waves
of ocean splashing against the ship's side.
It is more than a beautiful sight.
It is witnessing a shining glimmer
of God in His unflinching grace.

The morning is a loving embrace
of all that is good and wonderful

on this earth perched precariously
in a universe we try so hard to understand.
So much remains unclear, a mystery,
as we accept the soothing caress of God's glory.

COME WALK WITH ME
~ *To Kathy* ~

Come walk with me.
Let's walk the less used trails,
climb mountains, valleys explore,
where the wildness of nature still prevails.
Let's visit cultures of other lands,
share stories, and the people embrace.
Let's all join hands.

Come dance with me.
We will never despair,
be overcome by tragedy in life's wake.
We will grieve together and also celebrate
each day and joyful happenings make.
The people of each nation we will assure
human rights, coming together as we dance.

Come sing with me.
We will walk into the dazzling light
of hope, encouraging our sisters and brothers.
We will sing together lyrics from the heart
where music and song are forever understood,
while bringing the rhythmic union of dance
into the universal soul of humankind.

DREAM BEYOND BOUNDARIES

Dream those magical dreams.
You can climb heights never imagined
when persistence and hope abound.
Boundaries are set, it often seems.
when fear or lack of courage are unsound.

Raise the bar, your passions pursue,
Strive to be your personal best.

Worthy ambitions raise up high.
You'll conquer fear and no limits will ensue.
Move forward until you reach the sky.

No task will ever be too small.
No work will be demeaning
when honesty and integrity guide your way
while dreams are given your mighty all,
persistence and hope will carry the day.

❧

DON'T MISS A MINUTE
~ *To Adam* ~

"Hurry, Grandma, I don't want
to miss a minute.
Let's go to the movies.
get some popcorn and maybe a drink."
He looked up at me with those big brown eyes.
Yes, it's later than I think,
I began to realize.

21

I took his hand in mine as he sang happily,
"Hurry, Grandma, I don't want
to miss a minute."
Then I knew his favorite movie star
was probably in it.

These precious moments with my grandson
are rare and infinitely exquisite.
I hastily joined him in song.
"Let's hurry to the movies,
we don't want to miss a minute."

❧

THE CIRCUS IN OUR LITTLE TOWN
~ *To Robert* ~

The magic of the whistle across the distant plain
was the beginning of the week- long celebration,
announcing the arrival of the circus train,
in our lazy, sleepy little town.

I remember those days of childhood wonder
when the elephants and tigers marched
alongside the aerialists and sad-faced clowns
on their way to the circus camp grounds,
in our lazy, sleepy little town.

We children rushed through our morning chores,
hurried to the special set aside place,
where the bustling circus would be settling down.
The neighbors were all there to help raise
the huge tent, tugging and tying the ropes secure,
in our lazy, sleepy little town.

This was the biggest year-long event.
The outside world was suddenly brought
on the circus train, the kingdom
where acrobats, lions, music, and dance
became, for a week, part of the magical stance,
in our lazy, sleepy little town.

Looking back, I know it's been awhile
since the circus marched down the street,
and set up the tent. Now we have a magnificent
air-conditioned coliseum, always ready
for the magic of the outside world to come to the children
in our no longer lazy, sleepy little town.

Perhaps it is just a touch of nostalgic appeal
that comes over me as I excitedly watch
the animal trainer with the tigers and seals.
the beautiful girls riding horses performing tricks.

Through the eyes of an adult, the magic is still profound
remembering how it was in our little town.

ॐ

A DAY AT THE COUNTY FAIR

The day was suddenly aflame with light
as the dawn broke the darkness of the night.
Magic was in the morning everywhere.
Vicki and Jane awoke early for the County Fair,
rushing, getting ready their prized work,
sounds of laughter, giggles, and much mirth.

The fairgrounds and judges had come alive.
Youngsters had brought animals hoping for a prize.

A goat, a lamb, a chubby-faced pig,
A calf, a turkey, they all looked so big!
Bathed and scrubbed and shining clean,
the farm animals strutted looking so keen.

Vicki and Jane set up their exhibit,
thinking that all they could contribute
was a bundle of dresses, scarves, and skirts
they had made for 4-H. They looked so pale
in the presence of the cows, chickens, and rabbits,
until the judge came forth with the ribbon of blue.

A day of excitement for sisters Vicki and Jane,
each year the County Fair brings the children back again.

❧

I CELEBRATE LIFE

My eyes take in the sensual pleasures
of the golden sunshine and the beautiful flowers.
My ears bring me happy sounds to enjoy,
the singing of birds and laughter of the little boy.

I celebrate life while there is still time,
each cherished moment of the day is mine.

I lovingly touch the softness of the baby's skin.
I smell the freshness of the rain.
The clap of thunder doesn't bring fear,
but a spirit of love midst those who hear.
I celebrate the beauty of the poet's rhyme.
It is god's gift to man, noble talent divine.

ON THE FERRIS WHEEL

Children were shrieking sounds of fun
as the Ferris Wheel up and down spun,
flying way up in a circle all around.
Mother hoped the seats were securely bound
to the ropes that were attached to the ground.

Hold tight while the Wheel starts to spin.
A joyful sight, the signal to begin,
the hawker pushed the buttons up high.
The whirling and twirling toward the sky
were the biggest thrills for the passers by.

Looking to the left, another ride
was bouncing out of line to the side,
then climbed straight up several feet,
tossing the children in a scramble not neat,
upside down, then a jerk to beat.

Sounds of coins falling with a clang
hitting the metal on the wheel with a bang,
the children's pockets were emptied clean.
Mother breathed easier. After she had seen
such reckless rides, this Wheel seemed serene.

25

ALL ABOUT RESPECT
~ *To Trey* ~

The game starts at eight.
Eat breakfast and get ready.
"Hurry, Mom, we can't be late!"
Trey's child-like arms are steady
as he stretches over his head
his priceless jersey of blue and red.

Dad ran to start the car.
Close behind were Trey and Mom.
"Just come as you are,"
the coach says with aplomb.
He reminds the players not to miss,
"We will start the game," he insists.

"Soccer builds character,
play for the team,
learn good work habits,
keep your nose clean.
It is all about respect," they're told,
"Courage, honor and control."

The field is sparkling green.
The fresh dew is still damp.
Now the boys run so keen,
just like at summer camp,
to kick the soccer ball,
with luck, toward the goal!

"Our team won," the boys shout,
Trey made the goal at last."
They run and jump about,
"That makes our team the champs!"
Then Dad and Mom onto the field run,
"That is our soccer scoring son!"

❧

THE FRIENDSHIP TREE

I wake up at dawn,
one morning in May.
to the mockingbird's song.
What a wonderful day!

I jump out of bed,
ready for the fun,
can't be a sleepy head,
I'm on the run!

The last day of school,
we're going to the park,
swim in the pool,
get home before dark!

But before we do,
my third grade class
gave me some glue,
colored paper and task!

"Make a friendship tree
for teacher Sue,
we'll sign our names
all together in blue!"

"We thank you, Miss Sue,"
my heart beat wild.
"Goodbye for now,"
I managed to smile.

Her eyes seemed to dance,
she gave me a wink.
It might be just chance,
But the class didn't blink!

We sang our song
together in tune,
As we marched along
in the late May sun.

"We learned so much
from you, Miss Sue.
We'll miss your touch.
We all love you!"

NO TIME TO CHAT

Maybe it's important, maybe it isn't.
Why not? Let's give it a try.
Sign up for this. Sign up for that.
There's really no time to chat.
Just buy.

My son says it is serious.
My daughter says it is not.
How can I sort what's necessary
from the fast filling pot?
Just buy.

I turn on the television,
open the newspaper hoping to learn
what to do or where to turn.
My husband glances in my direction.
Just buy.

Oh, well, it makes for confusion.
As I try to sort the real from delusion,
my head starts to pound.
Coming to my senses, I finally rebound,
and refuse to buy!

Along the Way

THE JOURNEY

Yesterday I had an interesting dream
that I was going on a long journey.
This journey will be unlike any other.
There seems to be a destination
that will elude me for a long time.
Starting out seems pretty scary,
but I know it is a journey necessary,
one that I cannot escape or postpone.

I begin to see more clearly
many friends and events that have been
difficult to understand previously.
I feel reluctant to say goodbye.
Yet it is a task I feel compelled to complete.
Beautiful visions and moments divine
begin to envelope my nervous soul,
then the sadness, disappointments and tears.

My overflowing heart slows down
as I savor each joy as well as sorrow.
I am consumed by the peaks and shadows.
With surprising calmness I keep up courage
and continue this fascinating sojourn.
Foreign places are scarce, mostly the familiar
with even greater clarity
as I stay the course.

I open my eyes and try to shake this dream
of an inevitable journey.
What does this mean? Questions surround me.
Where is the destination? Where does it lead?

A joyous smile creeps into the essence
of my being as I am surrounded by
friends and family, mountains and valleys,
beauty incomparable.

❧

KINDNESS ABROAD

Kindness abroad,
Always a pleasure, enjoy your day.
So many civilities come my way.
Taking a tour down a Helsinki street,
Or climbing the Andes in a bus, we meet
Smiling faces, of all shades and hues,
A common language that chases the blues.

In all my travels abroad,
People welcome the mornings bright
Embarking on a journey into the light.
The natives may greet us with a dance
Often enticing us into a trance.
Each day is a gift to forever treasure,
Come what may, it's always a pleasure.

While traveling abroad.,
In Athens or Rome, whatever the weather,
Come along, let's celebrate this day together.
In Panama and Cancun we share the same song
Of canals in Venice or skyscrapers of Hong Kong.
From Hawaii to Vancouver, the welcome is there,
In palaces and castles the excitement we share.

❧

JOURNEY INTO THE PAST

Dipping into my barrel of memories,
I am reminded of kingdoms and dynasties
        now fallen by mighty armies
        centuries past. Ruins and scars
        dot the landscape as far as my eye
        can decipher. A Roman road of magnificence
            in its day now seems
        but a trail of stones in the distance.

What heroes fell, what heroes conquered,
        My imagination begins to swell.
        Days long past, gods and goddesses,
        Kings and princesses, legends of old
        So much to comprehend, so much to understand,
        Romance prevails upon the desert sand.
        I continue my travels in this foreign land.

❧

THE RUINS OF POMPEII

The whirlwind tour of foreign lands
        moved swiftly and surreal.
Rome and Florence flowed
        together with ruins, sculptures,
        and magnificent art from past centuries.

Pompeii stood out from the others,
        a buried city centuries old.
We learn about life, how people lived,
        worked and loved. Not very different
        from our lives today

❧

SIX DAYS AND NIGHTS

The shooting star pierces the night sky
and falls gracefully into the soaring
waves of dark water. All is calm.
Yet I must admit there is an uneasiness
I feel on my first Atlantic crossing.

I stare at the moving water while the great ship
parts the lingering waves
and sails along through the warm days
that tend to meld together,
and I lose track of time.

Six days and nights at sea,
time to reflect, time to meditate,
my life on land seems distant and unreal.
Old meanings fade and new ideas take their place.
The ship's gentle swaying rocks me to sleep

THE CRUISE CONTINUES ITS COURSE

He sat on the boat deck seemingly all naked skin
exposing his gigantic body to the sun's rays.
I wonder how he will obtain a tan
with the folds and layers concealing
huge areas of skin.

His coarse laugh and loud talk
are echoed by the wind overhead.
What kind of life, from where did he come?
Looking round I see that he is nor so different
from the other men on the boat.
A life of indulgence, pampered and spoiled,
is very evident by the opulence of passengers.

Six meals a day, endless dancing
and entertainment fill his days
as the cruise continues its course.

His reward for a lifetime of rushing,
meeting deadlines, making deals.
compromising, negotiating, making money
for the corporation. Now it is his turn.
His thoughts become confused, still one question
comes through. Is this what life is all about?

❧

CROSSING THE ATLANTIC

I step onto the deck of the beautiful ship.
The sun dips below the deep horizon.
Sapphire waves as high as miniature hills
are weaving and swaying and slipping
through the magnificent Atlantic.

I lean over and hold the rail
imagining, conjuring up intriguing secrets
being swept away by the ocean
as the grand ship makes its way through
the watery expanse into the starry darkness.

Looking overhead, I am hypnotized
by the night sky overflowing with stars
hanging so low I can almost reach out
and scoop them up into my menagerie
of stardust and dreamland.

Mysteries, heartaches, fears, and romance
are etched in the darkness of the night.

❧

OPEN THE GATE

The rocky coast, encircled in beauty,
invited my grandson and me
to go for a walk by the sea.
The waves were rushing onto the shore
as the tide came in once more.

We climbed the rocks, taking time
to savor the cool damp wind on our faces.
Slowly making our way to the lighthouse,
fragments of thought danced in my mind,
intriguing stories hidden along the jagged coast.

The lighthouse keeper of long ago
left traces of sorrow, piracy, and ploy.
What happened here is still unclear,
a young couple and their little boy
living together in the lighthouse yonder.

I could well imagine a time long past
when jaded lives in sorrow were overcast.
"Here, hold my arm, let's go inside,"
my grandson smiled. I could not say no.
Many disappearances before us, yet we decided to go.

"Don't be afraid, Grandma, dear.
Let's open the gate, I'm still right here."
"Uncommon courage, kindness to a stranger."
That was all I could decipher
on the small gravestone, still shrouded in mystery.

JOY UNCOMMON
~ *To Michael* ~

The sun was rising in a burst of splendor
Over the huge ship's bow.
Passengers nodded to each other as they drank vast
Amounts of coffee, tea and juice for breakfast.
An elderly lady walked out on the deck
Followed by a beautiful little boy.

This unlikely pair stood out from the throng,
Grandmother and child—engrossed in the beauty
And thrill of their first journey at sea.
The ports were inviting, each offering
Something unique to each tourist—a common experience
And a chance to develop a bond.

For this grandmother and grandson,
It was a special time—two children
(One in her second childhood) on an adventure.

Poets and writers try to capture the essence
Of love in many forms— sometimes romance, joy or fear.
Here, it was personified to all aware.
Love in its basic form, full of glory and awe,
Basking in dreams and joy uncommon.

ST. PETERSBURG

Extraordinary palaces, more than 200,
Adorn this city of many canals.
Magnificent museums, works of painters,
Architects and others dazzle and delight
The senses in the royal opulence of a culture
with opera and grand music.

A visit to St. Petersburg is like no other.
Going back to a time of Czars and Emperors
When palaces were built and given as a gift,
When enemies were destroyed by a hand's lift.
A history so different from North American,
Yet governments affected both ends of the earth.

Now the recovery of art and religion
Are being integrated into the democratic arena.
Much of the cultural and folkloric tradition
Can be seen in this new Russia.
The new generation struggles in the midst
of shaping a new ideology so vast.

❧

Traces in the Sand

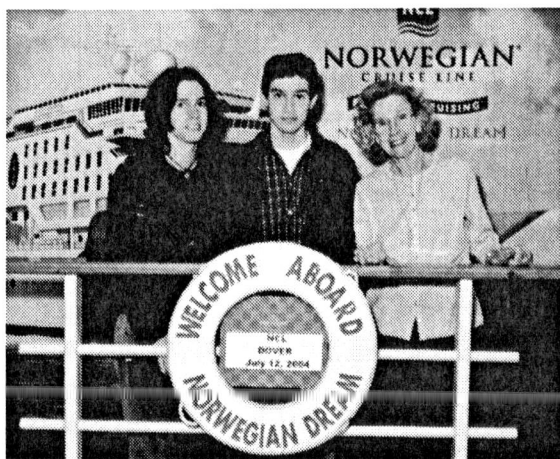

WINGS

She flew into my life on wings of hope
with a cock of her head and a flirty wink,
a joyful whistle mid colorful brilliance.
Dazzled, I was uplifted by the sight.

A touch of my hand, a smiling radiance
in her face, she was like a little bird
perched on my shoulder from far away
whispering words of encouragement.

Words often go unheard, lost in the wind.
Later they come back in a haunting song
of a bird in the treetops us to remind
ever so softly of a time long past.

One day she suddenly spread her wings
and with a cock of her head and a flirty wink,
again I was dazzled and she was gone.
In that moment I knew I had wings of my own.

Copyright 2004

POETRY IS BEAUTY

Poetry captures my spirit and my soul,
reflecting the images I behold
in dreams; beauty without season;
spirituality and loveliness without reason;
creativity beyond the boundary
erasing cacophony, bringing harmony.

43

Poetry is music for my song,
the peak of glory, surpassing splendor,
tumultuous joy, oft times depths of sorrow.

Poetry is love ethereal,
in praise of God, the Saints, the sky,
Heaven, the earth, and you and I.

Poetry speaks for my spirit and my soul,
reflecting the images I behold
in dreams.

❧

THE BEST OF TIMES
~ *To Daniel* ~

Singing in the early morning
as the sun rises over the neighboring hills,
looking eastward, the beauty of living
surrounds, enfolds, and uplifts my soul,
for family, love, and hope, forever grateful.

The poetry of an ever unfolding life
continues into the high noon.
I experience both excitement and contentment
as I eagerly look to the sunshine
and brightness of the afternoon.

Sometimes a halo of silvery light
shines through the expanding shades
of pastel and the richly imbued shadows
of early evening and late sunset.
Dreamily, I lift my head and dance into the night.

❧

EMBRACING THE NIGHT

Sadness creeps into the evening
while I struggle to recapture the day's joy.
Sometimes it happens so unexpectedly,
my inner resources are not working effectively.
I try to concentrate on my successes,
choosing to dismiss the downward spiral
of emotions caught in a continuous cycle.
Overwhelmed by the thought of tomorrow
I hold onto yesterday's sorrow.

The distant forest is forever beckoning
to my spirited heart in its search unceasing
for the loveliness inside the enchanted meadows.
I reach up and grasp the threshold of hope,
daring to step forward into the light,
out of past shadows and lingering sorrows.
I begin to sense the joyous tomorrows.
I hasten to close the chapter on yesterdays
as tranquility embraces the approaching night.

Copyright 2001

THE PINE CONE FAIR: A FANTASY
~ To Yvonne ~

Don't wake me if I am dreaming,
This is a fairy-tale place.
I hear red-breasted robins singing
musical notes of great beauty.
I see green and purple butterflies winging

45

azure blue and star dust yellow
through the fast moving waves of time
in the distance-filled splendor.

Don't wake me if I am dreaming,
This is a glory-filled place.
On my magical walk enchanted
by harmony and long sought peace,
The morning glory and honeysuckle pair
join in the nymph-like dance
of the birds and butterflies
at the Pine Cone Fair.

Copyright 1998

A VISION OF PEACE

Yesterday I had a stunning vision
of the world surrounded by love,
of children playing happily on the lawns
of neighbors, friends, and schools.
There was no distinction made by color,
handicap, age, or gender.
Laughter and joy were shining in the faces
of the children with no signs of fear.

A second look at the parents revealed
them making plans for future meetings,
serving the community in awesome ways,
helping each other get through trying days,
listening to the children as well as adults.
Sharing stories, caring neighbors were giving food
to the hungry across the land.
It seemed that a world at peace was at hand.

Reaching forth in an humble start,
I asked for permission to join the throng.
I wanted so much to be a part
of the crowds who were serving each other.
A welcome awaited me, I didn't hesitate.
We need your input, the world is at stake.
I held out my arms to the nearest child,
alone, but not lonely, she gave me a smile.

For such a day as this we say a prayer,
the magic of humanity has no boundary.
We are each other's keeper held together
by the bonds of circumstance and fate.
Let us join forces for the future and celebrate
the magical power of love, show no hate,
no fighting wars, just a world at peace.
There's hope when we come together and communicate.

꙰

THE COAL DUSTED TRAIL

Jennifer walked down the coal dusted trail
on an early November morning.
This was her daily difficult ritual,
to reach the small two-room school
in the swampy hollow of the rocky hill.

It was hard to finish the many chores
Dad and brother Charley had chosen
for her each morning before daybreak,
cooking breakfast, and lunch to make
ready as well as her homework.
Jennifer often wondered what it would be
like if Mamma were alive today

to help her and the family
through the hard times so lonely
as the coal mines were closing.

Thinking of the school day ahead,
she began to run in the warm
burst of sunshine on her quest.
"Education is my constant goal,
even a ten-year old can make things better.
Mamma would be proud."

The school bell began to ring
as Jennifer walked inside the door.
Head upright, she managed a grin,
"My turn has come," she glanced at the floor.
The teacher's smile made her spirit's soar
far from the coal dusted trail.

❧

CELESTIAL SPLENDOR

I gazed into the deep sky
looking for Hale-Bopp the comet.
The sun was setting below the horizon,
and the loveliness of the twilight
embraced me. Peering into the cloudless
heavens, I slowly became accustomed
to the starlit night.

Several constellations I could identify,
Andromeda, Cassiopeia and Perseus
in the Northwestern celestial splendor.
Searching with great anticipation,
I sat down to wait on the desert floor.

My heart took a leap as my expectation
suddenly turned into reality.

Spectacular beauty shining gloriously,
the head even brighter than the stars
trailing behind a long silver tail,
causing my senses to explode
in joyful wonder and uncommon magnitude.
I whisper a prayer.

Blessed am I to be in this place
on earth at this particular time,
to view the heavens through joy and tears,
to see what no human has gazed upon
for more than four thousand years.
Enchanted, I feel suspended in time,
somehow connected to my long forgotten ancestors
while launching into the future unknown.

Scientists will learn much about the creation
of the solar system from Hale-Bopp.
I will experience the glory and grace
of the comet on its journey
to the fringes of outer space.

☙

MAMMA'S KITCHEN TABLE

So much has happened here
at this weathered and scratched kitchen table.
As kids we all sat around
long after the meal was eaten
and the table cleared,
Doing homework with Mamma's guidance.

Wise words Mamma often spoke kindly.
Things seemed easier when she would say,
"Give thanks, finish your food,
do your chores and school work,
then we will make time for play."
Half the burden of childhood stress
her tender smile soothed away.

I press my hand along the deep scratch
of the kitchen table I so loved..
How can a thing so old and worn,
not polished and shining like Mamma kept,
but showing the cuts and scars made by children
long ago in their innocent quest,
be such a treasure years later?

Copyright 1998

THE DESERT TOWN

To tall green mountains,
and numerous cool trees,
I whispered goodbye to the lingering breeze.
Headed for the desert town,
sunshine and conditioned air.
Couldn't find a shady spot in the entire parking lot,
only a tiny shrub I found
left behind by the gardeners' fair.
Ninety days or so without rain
simply means I must again try
to endure the scorching pain of July!
Then in August, or maybe October,
clouds will darken the distant sky
bringing cooler weather for the brave souls
who last until November.

ON CLIMBING THE DESERT MOUNTAINS

The desert mountains stand oh, so still!
I gaze upon the sunset's colors bright.
My soul is touched by the thrill
of nature's way of showering light
on all her residents, large and small,
The animals as well as pine trees tall.

The desert mountains, how they soar!
Inviting us to their towering peaks,
I long for climbing just once more,
The sheer faced wall of stone I seek.
The challenge is there for me I know,
Yet, I continue to move so very slow!

I yearn for no more sadness and pain,
I must get past this hurtle to gain
peace of mind and love of man,
To reach out to others during my life span.
My needs are such that I can't see.
Come climb the desert mountains with me!

Copyright 1997

TEARDROPS IN THE DESERT SKY

"It's hot," visitors say.
"Don't come in summer.
The sun melts the sidewalk
with an unending array
of temperatures that soar,
and flaring tempers cause talk

to turn into yells and even a roar."

"Sometimes God takes pity
on this sun blistered city
and sheds some tears."
"The result?" the visitor asks.
Though not my task.
I attempt to explain

"A sky filled with teardrops
that bring cool rain
to the faithful residents
who stick it out
and don't complain."

✎

WAITING FOR THE CICADAS

This is the year of the cicada.
They're coming alright.
The signs are well in sight,
little holes in the ground outside.
For so many years they chose to hide,
now they are coming back to this land
to haunt us, causing much dismay.

Watch your children and your pets.
They'll come in hordes without delay.
Don't eat them, they'll make you sick
It's a curse upon our land,
There's nothing we can do, no known trick.
The old people's stories abound
as the bug-eyed children gather 'round.

This is the year of the cicada.
All the talk of war and fear,
the grown-ups have no time
to embrace the age-old mysteries
of nature and wonders of grace,
the longing for things so near,
even the shrill song of the cicadas.

꙳

A WHISPER OF WARNING

The sound of death, I had been told,
Was loud and eerie for many
        unfortunate souls.
Yet, I wasn't afraid.
Not that I was brave or bold,
I was just a bystander in this specter
        of pain and violence, going beyond
        the norm of decency
        for human behavior.

The sound of death I likened to a whisper
        of warning in the cold
        damp chambers of the streets
        on a darkened night.

53

It came out of alleys, the children
　　were the victims, unsuspecting,
Innocent, calling for their parents
　　who were not there
　　when the bullets of death
　　rang out in the night.

SHE TOUCHED THE SOOTHING SAND

The beach was encased in silence.
Walking alone, she dragged her feet
in the grainy, crunchy sand.
The tide came splashing in.
She moved to higher ground.

The cool dampness gave her pleasure,
away from the stifling sadness
of friends, family, and sorrow.
What had gone wrong was unclear,
the overwhelming feeling of horror.

A search into the past and future
brought no comfort of measure.
The cancer had caused her husband's death,
seemingly sudden and insensitive,
only days before her son's birth.

The beach was encased in silence
as the pain came in short intervals.
She touched the soothing sand.
She knew she must go back.
Slowly, she moved onto higher ground.

54

MAY I DANCE WITH YOU

"May I dance with you?"
a haunting phrase at my class reunion.
Sitting with my female peers
laughing and joking about past joys,
thinking of how much has changed these years
since the class play, sports, and senior boys.

We moved away from this little town.
went separate ways with marriage and careers,
launched out into the world on our own.
Life brought both happiness and pain
to each of us along the way

It was hard to recognize our friends
and others. A faintly familiar hand I felt
on my shoulder. "May I have this dance?"
A voice from many years past
echoed through the path of my memory.

I turned and there once again face to face
my childhood dream I could see.
"Andrew," I held out my hand.
"Do you remember me?"
Time has a way of standing in place.

"You gave me the homemade valentine
in Miss Simpson's class."
We laughed together that night divine,
reliving the awesome days of our past,
amazed at the childhood wonder we still felt.

"May I dance with you?"
a haunting phrase at my class reunion.
Sitting with my female peers

55

laughing and joking about past joys,
so much I had forgotten over the years,
but not this, no longer young, senior boy!

❧

TO WALK AWAY

Lifting the baby in her arms,
And taking her second son's hand,
She leaned forward and knocked
 on the heavy brown door of the shelter.

Why are they taking so long?
Why so slow? Please come,
It was hard to walk away.
Her strength and courage were gone.

"Hello," a soft voice spoke.
"Come in, my dear. Come out
 of the cold.
Here, let me take the child."

"We have a warm fire,
And food is on the table."
The kind lady smiled and
 led the way.

It was working. She had done it,
At last, she had walked away
 from the hell-filled house.
"An angel." She kissed the baby's face.

Copyright 1997

❧

Music in the Wind

DANCING IN THE MOON GLOW

Dancing in the moonglow,
Listening to the music in the wind,
Miraculous thoughts begin to unfold
In the deepening shadows of my mind.

The warm and ecstatic sensation,
In the midst of the wind's vibration,
Brings long unfelt thrills
As my spirit floats over the desert hills.

Dancing in the moonglow,
Listening to the music in the wind,
Cherished, childhood memories I bestow,
Comfort for the raging rivers in my mind.

Slowly drifting out of the night,
Back into the glare of the city's light,
I know that the miracle is there,
A symbol of hope for those who despair.

Copyright 1997

HALOS OF DREAMS FORGOTTEN

The twilight speaks in shadows
while the darkness my room embraces.
The night speaks in murmurs
of past thoughts and clouded memories.
At midnight, the chilling chimes
are reminders of lovers forgotten.

The early morning speaks in rhythms
bringing dawn's longed for lightness,
and the peaceful sleep patterns
erasing the eternal shades of sadness
with the brilliant colors of hope
encircling the halos of dreams forgotten.

MEMORIES UNRESOLVED

Confronted by images, both personal and universal,
Of humankind since the beginning of eternity
In the extraordinary evolution of time,
My mind searches for some scientific explanation
While my soul launches an adventure
Into the inner depths of exploration.

Sometimes joyous seasons of intense mystery,
Other times calm eons perpetuate tranquility,
My being immerses in travels exhilarating.
The haunting light appearing in the darkness
Of countless nights and in hovering skies
Conjures warriors in continuous surveillance.

Alas, visions and images of immense complexity
Summon my heart to capture the sublime beauty,
The days and nights of rhythm and harmony,
How it all comes together in wondrous balance
Of hate and love, despair and hope, joy and sorrow.
Deep in my heart, I know I will continue my search tomorrow.

STORM'S COMING IN

"Now, when I was a girl,"
Grandma often would say,
"Times were more calm
than they are today.
Just look at the storm
coming in from the East.
It's bringing more snow
with the skies overcast."

Grandma could almost always tell
by the snow birds' song,
and the distant church bell,
when something was wrong.
"We are in for hard times,
and it's not just the weather,
the crops will be small,
neighbors must pull together."

Her predictions were fair.
Grandma seemed so wise
as she braided her long hair
and looked into my eyes.
Silently, I sat enthralled
listening to her stories of the past.
The details she recalled,
"Snow will come,
but it will not last."

Grandma sits in her chair,
head tilted to one side,
her eyes aren't so clear,
she is less quick in her stride.
Just home from college,
I ask her with pride,

"What will it be like
for the family this Fall?"

"Now, when I was a girl,"
I heard grandma begin,
"We sat by the fire
when a storm came in,
told tales and sang a tune,
We'll do the same here."
I could tell by her tone,
it will be a good year.

※

GRANDMA'S VASE

The noise shattered the morning silence
as grandma's prized porcelain vase
fell to the much too close wooden floor.
In sudden fear, I rushed to my favorite hiding place
hoping to escape my grandmother's gaze.

"What was that? What did I hear?"
I shuddered and tried to make myself small
as Grandma came much too near.
When her footsteps faltered in the hall
there was no way for me to disappear.

Grandma looked at me under the curtain.
Please try to imagine the childhood fear
of a five-year old who has broken a vase
that her grandmother held dear,
and with no way to escape for certain.

62

"Come out sweetheart, accidents happen.
It seems it was meant to be.
We will clean it up after awhile,
give me a hug and sit on my knee.
It will be OK," she said with a smile.

Such fond memories of Grandma
come around often these days
and warm my heart in my old age.
Now that I am a grandma myself
I will try to pattern after her ways.

ॐ

IMAGES IN SILVER

Polishing the silver is such a chore,
can't think of much that I dread more.
Yet, it seems the task falls to me
as I plan the festivities that must be
each year to celebrate the holy holiday.
The grandchildren will come, safely, I pray.

Rubbing the soft cloth inside the tray,
my image appears in much the same way
it did as a child in yesteryear.
Startled, I polish without a smear;
this image seems foreign and not so clear.
White hair adorns my face, I fear.

I set the table on Christmas morning;
The turkey and pumpkin pies are baking.
I am reminded of my mother's holiday pleasure

as I excitedly place the shining silver
beside each grandchild's special plate.
White hair seems a blessing in my joyful state!

I RANG THE DINNER BELL

I rang the dinner bell clear and loud;
The heat was intense that summer day.
The farm hands looked toward the sun overhead.
They welcomed the meal with smiles along the way
as they walked the freshly plowed rows
of cotton, corn and beans now ready for the hoes.

Time has a way of moving very fast
   through youthful days of work and play
      when responsibility is for parents, at best.
        This long hot summer brings images that may
        conjure feelings of nostalgia long past.
        I look toward the sky today overcast.

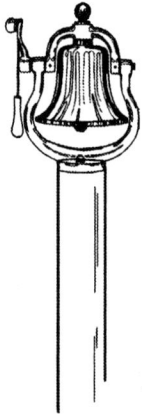

  The dinner bell no longer rings forlorn.
  but has rusted on its hinges way up high.
  My gaze lingers in the fields overgrown
  with weeds and trees reaching for the sky.
  Solemnly, I know the torch has been passed to me,
  taking care of the land is now my responsibility.

64

ON CLOSING THE F.W. WOOLWORTH STORE

Another end of an era sign,
the closing of Woolworth's five and dime.
I have been bracing myself for a decade,
knowing that a lot of changes would be made,
as I move reluctantly through middle age
and approach the new millennium.

Warm feelings come flowing into my heart,
while I remember the excitement of the times,
when mother and the kids dressed up and went
Christmas shopping at Woolworth's store.
We saved our money for doing chores;
could hardly wait for this magical shopping trip.

Searching the aisles, I saw so many bright
and glitzy toys. It was hard to select
for my sisters and brothers. A red spinning top,
I couldn't resist a dancing ballerina music box.
It was almost impossible to keep the gifts secret.
After all, it was a whole week until Christmas!

For mother, I felt so lucky to find
a sewing box and a ball of twine.
There were bows and fancy ribbons for our hair,
knit sweaters, and beautiful rayon underwear.
The counters were full of perfumes and jewelry.
Dazzled, I wished I had saved more money!

The pretty girl behind the cash register smiled.

"A perfect choice," she nodded pleasantly.
I knew right then that I wanted to be
an F.W. Woolworth clerk in my teens,
to enjoy helping others find lovely things,
the glitter and lights to feel and touch.

Mother said as she took us by the hand,
"Let's go to the counter and have some lunch."
The tantalizing smell of roasted peanuts and taffy
had taken their toll, and we were ready.
"A toasted cheese sandwich and a chocolate sundae."
For us children, nothing could have been more fun!

Prepare for change, it has had a long run,
the technological age is here we know.
Yet, somehow we feel a nostalgic glow
of sadness at the loss of things we hold dear,
the passing of an era, a childhood friend.
We solemnly watch the beloved Woolworth's disappear.

THE ALL DAY SINGING

The all day singing
was a special event
for family and fiends.
A Sunday well spent
at the little white church
along side the country road.

We sang gospel hymns,
then shared our food.
Dinner on the ground,
we invited the crowd.

A warm spirit of giving,
love, worship, and singing
permeated my being.

Images of yesterday,
the dancing memories
of joy and pleasures
in their own special way have become the treasures
a life time of searching have rendered my soul.
My heart continues
the all day singing.

TO DANCE AT THE CABARET
~ To Jane ~

When I was a toddler, a musical trance
filled our house as Father practiced the clarinet
in preparation for the Saturday night dance,
a world of enchantment down at the cabaret.
My mother taught me the waltz and swing,
while Dad kept time one-two-three-four.
I felt like an angel with brand new wings;
his foot kept tapping on the hardwood floor.

As a teen-ager, I wore bobby socks
to the school dances on Friday night.
I learned a new dance, the smooth fox trot,
 wore my trendy pink poodle skirt,
and listened to the sounds of the big band.
My father now sometimes played the trumpet.
His music was often in demand
at the schools, as well as the cabaret.

I grew up to be a young lady of class;
my father continued his music to play.
My mother could feel proud of me at last,
our dreams realized on my wedding day,
my father's big band sounds echoed the hall.
We danced until dawn,
an elegant night at the wedding ball,
the piano played softly; the memories were strong.

"Big Band Dance," I read the flyer
as we cruised along the highway
on our twenty-fifth wedding anniversary.
I closed my eyes remembering, sentimentally,
the long ago sounds of my father's horns,
the piano, the bass and the drums,
my mother's soft touch like a ricochet,
as we rounded the curve to the cabaret.

> *1997 Poet's Choice Award at*
> *International Society of Poets Convention and Symposium,*
> *Washington, D.C., August, 1997.*

RUN FORWARD FASTER
~ To Vicki ~

In the coolness of the morning dark
She saw dimly the trail's chalky mark.
As she began the long, long marathon,
Her feet settled into a fast beating rhythm.
Why had she committed to this run?
It was hard to justify it just for fun.

The stress of work and family, too,
Played a part she knew was true.
Unconsciously, she quickened her rhythmic pace,
Hoping for a break in the tightening race.
Run forward faster on the trail,
There's much at stake, set your sail!

There's no stopping the time flow,
The music has begun for the show.
She is soaring, flying, oh, so fast!
The feeling of ecstasy comes at last!
She sees the finish line up ahead,
It's easy now with no more dread.

Her feet are dancing, full of mirth,
It's hard to come back down to earth!
The clapping hands of family and friend
        signal to her that this is the end.
She knows she has done exceptionally well,
Silently, she waits for the results to tell!

Copyright 1998

MS. CHARDONAY'S FIRST DAY

Fresh out of college, I hoped I was ready.
Equipped with knowledge, I tried to keep steady.
In my shaking hand, the chalk wouldn't cooperate.
I could barely stand, my legs could scarcely operate.
My first day of school. I looked longingly at the class,
Boys and girls so cool, could they sense my jellied mass
        of tingling nerves and jangled thoughts?
I prayed for strength and calm.
Presence of mind I sought. Where was my soothing balm?

A hand went up so small, I managed a nod in my dismay.
"My name is Kate, my brother's Paul. We welcome you,
    Ms. Chardonay.
We've had no teacher for awhile, Ms. Harkins died late last
fall."
I saw a lingering tear, then a smile.
My heart signaled a call
    to my quivering body and jumbled mind.
Wake up, it's time to teach!
These children have needs of many kinds,
You have the means in your soul to reach!

HER SMILE WAS A PROMISE

The charm of the chimes ringing at seven
Enhanced and enlivened our rush to the classroom.
Expectant, familiar faces looked toward heaven,
From countries afar, with shattered dreams.
Adults, time worn, not children anymore,
Longing, yearning, so much to learn,
With hope for better worlds and a decent score,
A compassionate teacher with a kindly turn.

Her face seemed flushed midst our concern.
She moved in grace, her head held high.
Our fears increased.
Secrets would we learn of our new language?
We knew we would try.
Her smile was a promise from a line laced face
    filled with wisdom and hope
    in this magical place!

TO ADAM

Adam, my very special grandson, I miss you in many ways.
On our vacation we had fun. Now has past eleven days,
    and I sometimes feel blue.
I miss our breakfast rendezvous. You were in charge, alright!
Adam, you made me feel proud. Because of you,
    every day was a delight.

Things always went the way they should.
Memories, the best times of all,
    are spent with family, big and small.
Smiles and laughter in the sun, a time of hope
    and love to treasure,
Grandsons are always a pleasure.

FAMILY REUNION

At the stunning year of two thousand and three,
we decided to have a reunion, my family and me.
Plans were made for a covered dish at the park.
excitement and gaiety filled my heart.

My brothers and sisters, their families and friends,
were coming together after a long separation.
With many dreams and memories to share,
we launched the day with great anticipation.

It was good to get to know the nephews and nieces
who had beautiful children who were there.
"Who is this one?" Putting together all the pieces,
accomplishments and joys along with the sorrows.

Though years and space separated us a long while,
Family ties and love were strong enough to prevail.
We all shared tremendous pride on this special day
in the wonderful lives of each in his or her own way.

Two years later, the memories still clear,
I look toward heaven in solemn prayer and say,
"Thank you, Lord, for this blessed family so dear,
please bring us together again for a time very near."

SUGAR PLUM TREES AND DANCING PRINCESSES

Sugarplum trees and dancing princesses,
   ice with a mixture of snow,
   smells of pies filled with blueberries
all serve to remind me of a Christmas long ago.
Can you recall? Seems like, yes, it was Christmas Day

You were just little tykes in your pajamas
waking up in what seemed like the middle of the night.
nothing could contain you. Tony and I heard squeals of delight.
There was overflowing excitement on that morning long past.
We sensed the magic all around with innocence and merriment.

Little could we imagine that year ahead, what was in store,
on that fateful 60's day of yore. Not a hint of sorrow,
nor a cloud over tomorrow to dampen our hearts.
Life's journey took us along a rocky path, shattering dreams,
changing our course. Steadfast, we hung together, never apart.

What a beautiful memory of Christmas Day!
Tony dancing around with pretty princesses four,
wide-eyed and loving, they danced some more.
He was laughing and joking, bringing us cheer;
we were all looking forward to a wonderful year!

Almost forty years have come and gone.
It is a miracle how our family has grown.
Together we built a beautiful life so strong.
Robert came first; we were filled with awe.
He brought eternal music and forever joy.

Then came Daniel, a cute little busy guy,
Acting, dancing, full of surprises, a charming way.
Behold, Lauren appeared on a windy March day,
her little heart pounding and those big blue eyes
with tremendous appeal. Our lives were blessed.

73

Full of love, we didn't know there was room for more.
God surprised us and sent another baby boy!
Michael, cunning and grinning, we couldn't resist
His magical charms as he lay cuddled in our arms.
So playful and happy, hold me, he did insist!

Nineteen hundred and ninety, time does fly!
It was August, in what seemed like the twinkle of an eye,
another boy! Yvonne and Bob named him Trey.
His lustrous red hair and provocative ways
stole our hearts during those very warm days.

Each Christmas we pause to think of our past,
the paths we have taken, directions we've chosen.
Always separate, distinctive, intelligent,
Aspirations high, success to treasure, still a family together.
Who would have thought it ever could be?

On the third of May, nineteen hundred and ninety-four,
"Someone new," a message came as if by chance,
"has come. A baby has entered our lives once more."
We looked at each other, and then at Adam.
He's full of life, we could tell at a glance.

Kathy and Dave, you've brought us another.
We are thrilled. He brings excitement as he begins to chatter.
Always talking and laughing, such brilliant personality,
we just know he will grow up to be a philosopher!

Over the years God blessed us with Bob, Dave, Tim, and Doug,
then Audrey, a lady fair, very elegant, with auburn hair.
Today, as I look around and see my beautiful family,
I am reminded of sugarplum trees and dancing princesses.
These memories will always bring us pleasure.

※

FORCES RANDOM

The lady turned her face to the wind,
gazing toward the rising waves
as the ocean changed its colors
with fickle fancy in the face of the storm.

Time seemed of the essence
in this moment of rising suspense.
Were others in danger along the coast?
Or just the incoming vessels
bringing loved ones to the shore?

Time may change the faces,
 fade the vividness of the memories,
circumstances alter lifelong plans,
dreams often shattered by forces
random, and uncontrollable by man.

The lady turned her face from the wind,
a lone tear trickling down the furrows
left by rising waves of sorrow, disappointment and fear.
Soft as the morning sea, she whispered in my ear,
 "It was such a storm
as this that took my love from me."

Copyright 2000

The Wheels of Time

THE WHEELS OF TIME

Sitting in the fast moving train in reverie,
without listening, the wheels bring echoes.
I am reminded of a childhood journey,
backward in time my thoughts meander.

Mom sat in the seat just ahead
with my little sisters at her side.
Mom seemed so brave to me as a child,
I could look around almost unafraid.

What the future held, I could only wonder.
Going to live with cousins so far,
 Mom explained as an adventure.
Dad's death had brought change as well as sorrow.

A sudden jolt as the train began to slow,
we were coming into the little station
that I remembered so well from long ago,
another goodbye, this time to Mother.

REVERSAL

"Come down for breakfast!
Hurry up, don't be last!"
I called through the years,
"Get ready for school, my dears."

The stairway was crowded with running feet
as they rushed to the kitchen all upbeat.
Laughter and giggles filled the morning air,
though the food was scarce with none to spare.

Coats and hats, mittens and books
were given to each child with loving looks.
They passed inspection on the way to the bus,
leaving the nest, without a fuss!

"Come down for breakfast!"
I hear my daughter call. Alas!
Time has brought a generation's reversal.
Finding my cane, I rush to meet her approval.

I STROLL THE SUNRISE

I walk the moonbeams,
then dance the sunset
and stroll the sunrise.
The beauty of God's world
totally serves to energize.

Awakening from my night dreams,
I eagerly face the morning.
The whistle of the six o'clock train
pierces the silence, once again
capturing a glimmer of the light of day.

Moments of enchantment along the way,
sacred scenes of mountains and green trees,

bright faces of flowers and buzzing bees,
the splendor of God's world
totally serves to inspire.

❧

ON AGING

The echoing depths of the night
are ever present in my heart.
Both the sounds and the stillness pervade
the minute spiral of twilight
in the mourning of my soul.
conquering the bounds of time complete.

I take cover into the exhilaration
of the beauty and the joy of daylight.
There is so much left in life to embrace.
Yet my dance with time continues
far beyond the melody of the night.

❧

I LOVED YOU THEN

"Love," she murmured, "is so fleeting.
My first glimpse of your face retreating
into the shadows of childhood time
is forever etched in the niches of my mind."

"I loved you then, you couldn't know.
We seemed worlds apart even though
our desks were separated by the narrow aisle
that I easily measured as more than a mile."

Touching his hand after so many years,
The lovely lady hoped behind her tears,
Searching for a glimmer of the passion of the past.
"You couldn't know," she whispered, alas!

※

DREAMS ARE MY CONNECTION TO YOU
~ *A SONG* ~

When you left I thought my world
had come to an end.
I felt so sad, so disconnected.
I dreaded the night when sleep wouldn't come.

Chorus
Then I was given a magical dream
filled with beautiful memories of you.
Dreams have little value ordinarily,
but they are my connection to you.

Tears flow easily throughout the day.
Friends say, "Come on, let's go out,
have some fun, help you forget.
Life goes on for the strong."

Chorus Repeat
Eventually, my friends all say
I won't have much pain.
Someone new will come into my life again,
But in my heart I know

Chorus Repeat

※

SHADES OF JOY

The sudden burst of color so bright
over the green hills in the fading light
of a summer day awakens
the senses. God's glory shining
in the many shapes and shades inspire
humankind with joys quite stunning.

Images of angels, streets of gold,
the heavens open the depths of my soul.
God's everlasting love, same as of old,
shining through the sadness at end of day,
the colors of magic and miracles bold,
bring only beauty and shades of joy.

NOT SO FAR AWAY

Sadness moved across the stranger's face
seeping downward into her neck's purple veins.
Her chest picked up the deep emotion with a sigh,
the tightening and gasping were keenly felt.

Tourists moved quickly through the foreign place,
not willing to look into the stranger's hollow eyes.
One lone lady to the side gave a glance,
alarmingly aware of the wounds and the pain,
shaking her head as if to say, "Not again!"

Then the military vehicle drove so very near
as the victim was loaded into the Red Cross van.
Memories of childhood hiding and paralyzing fear
came to haunt the one visitor aware.

Catching up with her friends on the beaten track,
she quickened her step and forced a grin,
"Another world this woman lives in!"
What surprised her most was she dared to look back.

❦

THE MISSING SKYLARK

On a misty morn dim and dark,
I sat out to find the missing skylark.
It was known by all the common folk
that time of day could hold the key
to nature's coquettish and fickle link,
while hiding the best of the songbirds from me.

The rain fell harshly on my face.
it seemed vain and almost commonplace.
Callous, yet splendid, the droplets trace
cavern and canyon down the terrace
with a trickle, like tears, slowly settling
on where the missing bird was singing.

Morning rain, warm and sensual,
led me here to this sensational
twisted, weather worn tree.
No longer subdued by the dim and dark misty morn,
nature's frolicsome secret I had uncovered,
the missing lark with babies three.

❦

AN ALMOST INAUDIBLE ECHO

It doesn't seem like much to ask,
A handshake, a nod of recognition.
Yet overwhelming seems the task
for those on the periphery of oblivion.

Away from family, foe, and friends,
I awaken in the strange and foreign town,
No beloved to soften the disharmonious blends
of unfamiliar sights and callous clowns.

What can I do, I begin to wonder,
To melt these layers of uncaring crust?
Searching, I hear in the starlit splendor
an almost inaudible echo, "Go forward, trust!"

Copyright 1998

A MOMENT OF SERENITY

I look into the vast chasm of eternity,
My gaze focusing on the cathedrals, monoliths and temples
shaped by the erosion of wind, and the rivers of time.
Millions of years have brought me this moment of serenity.
The Grand Canyon is more than a monument.
It evokes the feeling of writing an immortal sonnet
describing what it is like to look upon God's face.

The depth of the beauty pierces my soul.
I am exhilarated by God's embrace.
The sunrise and sunset bring added dimensions

of brilliant colors, purple shadows and variations.
Only the Native American tribe living on the canyon floor
have experienced this unrivaled magnificence
for centuries. Time moves on adding more glory.

࿐

PROCEDURAL PREPARATION

The voice sounded detached, distant, and disowned.
"Your mammogram shows an abnormality
which needs to be investigated further.
Do you have a preferred surgeon?"

Her mind reeled with questions,
so many things left unsaid. What is the prognosis?
What happens after the surgery?
Set up the appointments, the schedule.

"It is just a small lump, may not mean much,
but must be removed to make a treatment plan."
The fear, the horror of it all,
        no one takes the time to listen.

The measuring pin point
        in the lab procedural preparation,
cold hands, blunt needles, breathless expectation.
"Take her blood pressure,."

"It's cold in here. Bring a warm blanket."
Her shivering body seemed to calm
as the anesthesia took over
        and sleep came mercifully.

86

"Wake up," a voice across the space
came crashing through the silence
    of near death transition
back to the present and harsh awakening.

The painful, cruel aftermath of vomiting and not knowing,
the internal bleeding and suctioning,
When will peace come?
The trip to the surgeon's office.

"You are one of the fortunate few
    whose growth is benign."
A swell of relief in the burning chasm of bruised soreness
and missing sections of breast tissue.

A look in the mirror brings sorrow and mourning,
though thankful for modern medicine ,
a grateful prayer
    midst triumph bittersweet.

THE OLD MAN WITH THE VIOLIN

Bending his stooped shoulders, he picked
up his scratched and much used violin
from the rickety mantle above the fireplace.
His half-closed eyes sparkled and his lips pursed.
With shaking hands and wobbling knee,
he pulled the bow across the key.

I had heard of this aged man
who lived alone in a mountain shack,
a musical legend from long ago,
not conquered by time and much bad
   luck.

He seldom ventured beyond the valley below,
said those who knew him before the 50's flood.

The music came flowing as lustrous as silk
with sounds and beats in soothing streams
awakening my memory of childhood dreams.
Resting my head on the back of the chair,
my senses were tingling with delicious pleasure.
The old man with the violin had touched my soul.

 &

BE WARY, CHILD

The watermelon looked deliciously tempting.
Sitting on the park bench apart,
in the shade of the massive oak,
I watched the young boy's face
get buried in the red juicy heart
of the dark and light stripes alternating.

Peering up at me from the tantalizing rind,
the smiling eyes seemed puzzled, but unafraid.
"Mom, may I share my melon?"
"Hush, and eat," she admonished the child.
I turned my face toward the shadows.

 &

ALONE ON THE PATH

Love, hope, dreams, and passion,
Where have they gone this gloomy day?
Hearts, music, ribbons, and flowers

seem distant while awaiting the arrival
of the news of possible survival
in the aftermath of the bloody showers.
Will anyone travel again the road this way?
I walk alone on the path now beaten.

ॐ

IN THE SILENCE OF THE DAWNING

In the silence of the dawning,
I sometimes pause momentarily
to reflect on my life spanning
well over two-thirds of the century,
both the progress and the turmoil, experiencing
technical and social change intensely.

The twentieth century had its days,
memories of hard times, the depression,
.much work, and families pulling together,
railroads and trains filled with runaways.
While two world wars were fought for humankind
the glimmer of freedom served to bind.

Against contagious diseases immunization,
the introduction of purification and sanitation,
advances in medicine and proper nutrition,
knowledge of health habits and lifestyle,
exercise, stress managing
have extended joy and life expectancy.

So many twenty-first century predictions,
America welcomes new ideas. Amazing discoveries
 in science and treatment for body and mind

will take on cutting edge dimensions.
Midst conflicts in space, and travel through time
the glimmer of faith will serve to bind.

૪

ON THINNING HAIR

Now that I am advancing in years,
and my eyesight is becoming dim,
don't pity me with your tears.
Stop and visit for awhile.
Ask about my past on a whim,
that will bring a smile.

I've lived a hard wild life
full of adventure and romance,
always willing to face up to strife,
daring to venture into the future,
yet never turning aside the chance
to tell a funny joke, have a good laugh.

As for regrets, I haven't any . . .
just maybe not marrying Tom or Sam.
Quite the contrary, there were many
good men, or so they said,
asking for my lady like hand
when I was young and pretty.

Why I chose to marry Les,
my mother questioned with aplomb.
Looking back, it's hard to guess,
except for his bright eyes and curly hair.
Everyone said he was just a bum.
Nevertheless, for life he had a flair.

90

Now that Les has gone to rest,
with fading eyesight, available men, I assess.
Every day, trying to look my best,
the men I meet are bald or thin.
Since hair is no longer my concern
no more do I face them with chagrin!

✄

THE HAUNTING IMAGE

She moved along the street
    in slow motion, it seemed to me.
Her head was nodding barely,
Her shoulders slumped ever so slightly.
There was something familiar vaguely,
Although just what I couldn't recall
    as I walked through the narrow road
    searching for my condominium so small.

There were many old women around
    walking the streets alone, seemingly
    no where to go, no where they belonged.
This tragedy played itself out in my mind,
    day after day in this hostile land,
Yet this image seemed separate, haunting.
Touching my face, my hand felt a tremor,
One and the same, I recognized in the mirror.

Copyright 1998

✄

91

Softened Silence

SOFTENED SILRNCE

Loving you brought softened silence
    over lonely roads, and shortened the distance.
Early hour before the sunrise walking
    through the neighborhood city park,
We saw little need for senseless talking,
Being with you served to fade the dark.

Countless days have moved endlessly
    through the ever changing seasons.
The years added up seeming effortlessly.
Raising the children strengthened our reasons
    to love in difficult times. Later prosperity
    brought thankfulness and much happiness.

Loving you brought softened silence
    over lonely roads, and shortened the distance.
Now early hours before the springtime dawning
I walk alone through the neighborhood city park,
Wishing you were here for senseless talking
    before my world collapses in the dark.

WAITING FOR THE DAWN

Day light and shadows,
Day dreams and meadows,
Faded by the tapestry of time.
Remembering past love sublime,
Alone, teardrops, heartfelt,

95

Fall on tissues, hand held,
While waiting for the dawn
    with no solace in between.

"Love, unconquerable," she once said,
As she lifted his motionless head
    from the satin casket pillow,
"Knows no earthly barrier."
Now she seemed hypnotized by the candle
    flickering in silence,
While waiting for the dawn,
    with no comfort in between.

THE MORTAL PARTING

In the spring of your life
our eyes met in glorious wonder.
A magical spell was cast,
youthful dreams of splendor
and romance fulfilled and blessed.

The entire earth sang and danced
on our enchanted wedding day.
We were transcended, entranced.
"Such happiness is rare,
in even the most sacred way,
and reserved for the immortal,"
I whispered without a care
to the strains of our wedding march.

The years went past in a windswept flurry.
Days turned into nights so fast-paced, exciting,
always in a hurry to do more, to see more,

to be more, to love more.
You, I did adore!

Death came for you so sudden.
I was not prepared to live
in the desolate void of separateness.
Now I whisper to the strains
of the angel's chorus,
"Such happiness is rare and reserved
for the immortal."

ॐ

STAY AWHILE

Don't leave me now,
Please stay awhile.
The darkness surrounds
   and brings more tears.

Don't leave me now,
Please stay awhile.
The dawn will come soon
   and soften my fears.

Don't leave me now,
Please stay awhile.
It's hard to say goodbye
   after so many years.

Don't leave me now,
Please stay awhile,
She whispered in the dark.
God took him just before light.

ॐ

SPRING GARDEN OF ROMANCE

It was early spring, our hearts entwined,
when humming birds and butterflies
enjoyed with us the fragrant four-o-clocks,
with red, pink, yellow and white
mingled with spires of hollyhocks.

It was late spring when romance began to unfold.
Splendid sweet peas and blue bells enhanced
our love, dazzling to behold.
Roses, marigolds and blooming trees
reminded us of lonely days foretold.

Spring is over. Death came too soon.
My heart now beats in a rhythmic measure.
Saddened I hum a somber tune,
while memories of days of pleasure
haunt my garden of romance and you.

৵

A CHILDHOOD MORNING

I saw my mother's face shining
intensely with her love's bright glow.
It was an early November morning
when a light feathery snow
had brought the chilling wind
and the early signs of winter.

Mother's voice took away my fear,
as she hummed a soft lullaby to me.
I knew all that we held dear

was safe after the storm. You see,
the clock on the mantle was ticking
rhythmically, and, again reassuring,
like the sounds of my mother's heart.

ℒ

SUNDAY AT GRANDMA'S

All week I looked forward to Sunday,
when we dressed up in our best,
and drove to Grandma's house
where everything was always special.

Grandma welcomed us with arms outstretched.
Mother's younger sisters were there, too,
looking so pretty in pink and blue,
patting our cheeks and giving us love.

Grandma's house had peace and a kind word,
although times were not easy, most often hard,
during the Great Depression of my youth
when clothes were handed down with a patch.

Food was scarce, but we always shared.
As kids, we knew we were blessed very much,
daring to dream and look ahead
with Grandma and aunts and loving hearts.

We learned the lessons of doing good deeds,
and basic truths, helping others in need
with never any thoughts of selfish greed.
Remembering Grandma and my aunts, I give thanks.

ℒ

COME FOR TEA

Her eyes were less bright,
Her frail frame fragile and limp,
As she hovered in the lingering light
    of the slowing sinking lamp.

"It's your sister who is here
to visit and have a nice talk."
The caregiver said with an austere
    demeanor and a helpless look.

I rushed to her and tried to smile.
I had dreamed of this place
    as I drove that last mile.
Leaning forward, I kissed her passionless face.

"I brought milk and a tea cake,"
I opened the small bag of food,
"Just like Mother used to make.
Let's eat, and maybe pretend."

My sister turned and looked straight at me,
"Let's have a tea party,"
She whispered in almost glee.
"Like when we were kids," I spoke softly.

Copyright 1997

100

I PLANTED SPRING FLOWERS TODAY

I planted spring flowers today.
There were geraniums, daises and roses
To set out in the warm moist earth.
It was a wondrous, exciting way
To celebrate the dawning of spring's mirth.

Standing back looking with admiration
At the marvel and miracle of birth,
I saw that God's handiwork
Was full of sparkle and imagination
That was not possible to emulate.

My thoughts traveled to an earlier morning
When my sister and I picked posies
On a spring day sparkling like this.
The wild flowers were dazzling and alluring,
Not one white daisy did we miss!

My flowers today are just as lovely,
Yet I sense there is something amiss.
My eyes look into the far distance
Where my sister's grave lies in the cemetery.
Across the daisies I blow a kiss.

Copyright 1997

COUNTRYSIDE MOURNING

She had been my friend for a long time.
   It was hard to remember when
our childhood friendship actually began.
Always there with a willing ear,
eager to listen and to share
 sorrow as well as joy.

The phone call came as a surprise.
Her death was a jolt in my life.
I had not heard about the cancer
that had invaded my friend's breast,
an abrupt intrusion in a life cut short
with dreams unfulfilled.

I drove along the countryside serene,
noticing things I had not seen
for many years. Pink and white dogwood,
sparkling clear water trickling down a hillside.
These were the scenes we so often enjoyed
as childhood friends.

Would her funeral be fitting
for a woman so bright,
full of laughter and spirit
that could outwit the prevailing fad,
live a life pushing the boundaries,
dreaming the heights?

The strains of the old-fashioned hymn
drifted out the little church door.
"Amazing grace," what a perfect tribute
for my childhood friend's farewell

as she moved through the twilight
to heaven's path,
past the countryside mourning.

ঽ

WHEN IS DADDY COMING HOME

"When is Daddy coming home?"
Her youthful voice touched my heart.
My hand reached out for my fragile child,
"Come sit with me," I made a start.
Holding her close, if only for a short while,
I hoped would soothe her saddened soul.

"When is Daddy coming home?"
The words were spoken in a plea.
She seemed to sense my hesitation
to speak the truth about her destiny.
As I searched in desperation,
I prayed to God her spirit to strengthen.

"When is Daddy coming home?"
Her words echoed the intricate pain
from deep within my being.
How can a mother hope to explain
that Daddy won't be coming home again?

Copyright 1997

ঽ

103

Acknowledgements

"Forces Random," in *America At The Millennium: The Best Poems And Poets Of The 20th Century* © 2000 by The International Library of Poetry. All rights reserved.

"I Stroll The sunrise," in *As Sunlight Wanes* © 2000 by The International Library of Poetry. All rights reserved.

"Embracing The Night," in *Poetry's Elite: The Best Poets Of 2000* © 2001 by The International Library of Poetry. All rights reserved.

"Joy Uncommon," in *The Best Poems And Poets Of 2001* © 2002 by The International Library of Poetry. All rights reserved.

"Memories Unresolved," in *The Best Poems And Poets Of 2002* © 2003 by The International Library of Poetry. All rights reserved.

"October's Shadows," in *The Best Poems And Poets Of 2003* © 2004 by The International Library of Poetry. All rights reserved.

"Birdsong And Child," in *Theatre Of The Mind* © 2003 by Noble House Publishers. All rights reserved.

"Late September," in poetry.com/Publications © 2004 by The International Library of Poetry. All rights reserved.

"Wings," in *The International Who's Who In Poetry* © 2004 by The International Library of Poetry. All rights reserved.

Printed in the United States
24153LVS00001B/64-87